JUMP START YOUR JOY

HEART-CENTERED WAYS TO FIND JOY IN THE MESSY MIDDLE

Paula Jenkins

Jump Start Your Joy: Heart-Centered Ways to Find Joy in the Messy Middle

Published by Welcoming Spirit Press

Paula Jenkins/ Welcoming Spirit Press
Jump Start Your Joy ® is a Trademark of Paula Jenkins

Ordering Information:
Quantity sales. Special discounts are available on quantity purchases by corporations, associations, and others. For details, contact the "Special Sales Department" at the email address above.

Jump Start Your Joy: Heart-centered Ways to Find Joy in the Messy Middle/ Paula Jenkins. —1st ed.
ISBN 978-0-578-81377-6

Be like the bird who,
pausing in her flight
on limb too slight,
feels them give way beneath her,
and yet sings,
knowing she hath wings.
-Victor Hugo

Dedicated to my mother, Sally Jenkins

TABLE OF CONTENTS

CHAPTER 1 7

CHAPTER 2 13

CHAPTER 3 21

CHAPTER 4 27

CHAPTER 5 35

CHAPTER 6 43

CHAPTER 7 49

CHAPTER ONE
Inspiration, Intention, and Action

"Follow your joy. Always. I think that if you do that, life will take you on the course that it's meant to take you." – Jonathon Groff

When I used to be asked what I wanted to be when I grew up, I remember answering with just one unexpected word: Happy.

This answer made people at my dad's company picnics chuckle, and chatter back and forth saying, "Isn't that sweet? The innocence of youth." The silent ones tended to give me looks that made me feel like I was doing something wrong. The message was that you are supposed to say what you want to DO, instead of describing how you want to feel.

Fast forward to forty years later: I now see that a desire to "be happy" as the starting point for a connection to something bigger, and much more sacred than our momentary feelings and emotions. It is a desire to return to a connection with joy, to reconnect to our true nature, and to be aligned with our purpose here on Earth through a deeper connection to our spirit.

At our core, I believe each of us wants to be connected to the higher vibrational emotions of joy, delight, and love because it is inherent to our natural wiring. We arrive here at birth connected to the positive emotions and feelings. We slowly unlearn how to connect to that side of ourselves during life. And still, the desire to reconnect with joy, delight, and love never leaves us. We each want to know that we can connect with joy, and I believe all of us want joy to be woven into our daily existence.

As a self-proclaimed rebel, and modern-day trail blazer I'm more than delighted to share that forty years later, joy is at the heart of all that I do. I started the podcast "Jump Start Your Joy" in 2015. The heart of the show is exploring how people choose joy, even during hard times and difficult situations. I look at how joy and love often come looking for us, inviting us to reconnect with our authentic nature, even when we are in those overwhelming places in our lives. The show has taught me many things, having spoken to hundreds of people about how they have jump started joy in their life, in the world, and in other people's lives.

As we are growing up, messaging from outside of ourselves begins to influence what we think we "should" do, be, believe or pursue in our lives. It is a long, slow shift from being rooted in joy and connection as an infant, knowing that you want to "be happy" as a child, to finding yourself detached from your intrinsic joy as an adult. You may hear the shoulds from grownups at company picnics as a child, from "mean girls" in high school, from an overbearing boss, or more subtly from "gurus" on the internet or social media ... but somewhere along the path into adulthood, we shift into the belief that "doing" is so much more important than "being." And we lose the connection to our truth, our joy, and often, our purpose.

Without much thought or any fight, we morph into people who prize accomplishments, accolades, and head pats. Like me, maybe you became the A student and applied to the good schools and got a great internship at a well-known company, and then went on for another degree. Maybe you have put all your time and energy into starting a company, raising children, or being the best at something in your field. These are all noble pursuits.

Here is the thing. Just based on the fact that you are reading this little book, I know something else about you.

Even in the face of hard things, even when you are afraid, even when you are not sure what the future holds, you know that you also want *more*. You recall the connection you had to your own true spirit. You want to reconnect with the goodness of the universe. You want to rekindle that, and you want to figure out how to jump start it in your life. I want this, too. I want it for you, and I want it for the world. Because the more of us who choose joy and share joy and create joy in the world, the better we all feel and the healthier we all will be.

The Journey to Joy

In 2015, I took the leap to follow the muse of joy and launch a podcast that I thought would be the marketing arm for a life coaching business. I was completing a life coaching certification and had been fascinated with podcasting for years.
Joy, and the universe, had other ideas for me and my podcast. I have found that this is often what happens when you align yourself with your true center and reconnect with joy: things start to fall into place in your life because you are reconnected with what lights you up.

Friends started inquiring how I created a podcast and asked me to help them do the same. Now, five years later I have the "perfect" job (for me) doing an unconventional and rebellious mix of podcast producing, project management, and life coaching. I love what I do, and it all started with me looking for ways to jump start my own joy.

This tiny book is all about how you jump start joy and reconnect with your own spirit and wholeness. In hard times and difficult situations, choosing joy makes all the difference. You can make the choice now to "grow up" to be not simply happy, but truly joyful, feeling connected, and in touch with your sacred alignment. Choosing joy Is a part of that path.

A Framework for Joy

Over the years, I have created a framework on how to approach joy and bring more of it into everyday life. In my work as a life coach, I have heard many people say "I don't know what I enjoy anymore," or, "I don't have time to do 'frivolous' things like play or goof around."

As a society, we are not taught to value joy, or to make room for it in a sacred way. I believe that joy is sacred, and offers us a connection to something bigger than ourselves, something that reminds you of who you were before you arrived on this plane of existence. To reconnect with joy, you will need to reflect on what that means for you: If you are religious, you may interpret that as an energetic connection to God, the Creator, or whatever Deity is sacred to you. If you are of more of a spiritual leaning, you may sense a connection with the universe, the collective whole, and the energy of the cosmos. And for all of us (agnostics, included), joy connects us to what is truly sacred to our inner landscape. Joy is a through line for what is important to us, what we align with, and what feels closest and dearest to our hearts.

The trouble is, as important as joy is, it gets pushed aside. The world will tell us there is something more important than slowing down to experience joy. Getting reacquainted with joy and inviting it in can take a mindful approach. This is how I've come to talk about it on my show:

Inspiration: What inspires you? Author Wayne Dyer says that "inspiration" is also another take on the word "in-spirit." When you are inspired, you are drawn to something that sits very close to your deeper purpose, or your inner source. I think of inspiration as the guideposts for what lights up your soul, and what you were sent to the Earth to do. And, I believe that noticing what inspires you, and mindfully bringing more of that into your life is joy's way of inviting you to come and play with it, and to reconnect with your true self.

Intention: In this framework, intention is mindfulness. Once you have noticed what delights you and know that you want to bring more of it into your life, you set the intention to do just that. When you have the desire to bring more joy and happiness into the world, it's important to be intentional and focused on your task because it's very easy for those things that inspire us to remain ethereal, or to remain on a bucket list for years. We have received too much messaging that signals us that "doing" is the more worthy and measurable pursuit. To return to joy, we need to be mindful and conscious about our approach.

To bring joy and wellness into your life, you must become intentional with your focus and your time on that thing. Being mindful of your desire for joy and your desire to take an active role in creating happiness for yourself is all baked into the idea of intention. Being inspired is lovely. Intention helps to connect that inspiration to the action you take to bring your own joy into the world. And it helps mindfully connect you with your creativity, and aligns you with your purpose, all by focusing on what joy looks like for you.

Action: Taking action, making the time, and doing things that bring you joy (or allow you to feel connected, fulfilled, or whole) is the way you bring that joyful intention into your life. Action is where you take what inspires you, apply your mindfulness, and do something that feels good or joy filled. It may also mean noticing what is missing in your life (which we will explore later), and taking steps to re-integrate those things, or, it might mean that you reach out for help if you feel overwhelmed or need support.

Without consistent action, things remain undone. Without setting aside mindful time to interact with joy, or take steps to return to a joyful state, it remains in the ethereal space of "I wish" or "I'll do that when..." Action, even with tiny baby steps at 15 minutes at a time will create space and time to nurture joy and reconnect you with your spirit.

A jumping off point, as you start to jump start your joy:

Take an inventory of what brings you joy, now. What in your daily life connects you with your inner source and wellness? Name as many things as you can.

How are you hard wired? What is at the core of who you are? What is your relationship with joy?

What is your messy middle? What does your current reality look like?

CHAPTER TWO
The Messy Middle

The messy middle is a time of transformation. You cannot have growth without growing, just as you cannot have a beginning or an ending without a middle.

How do we find joy when things feel weird, mixed up, or difficult? What does it look like when we are faced with "The Messy Middle?"

For the scope of this book, I define the messy middle as the times in our lives when things feel weird, mixed up, or difficult. It can be the result of large events in our lives, like the pandemic (which is what inspired me to dig deeper on talking about how to find joy during the messy middle), or it could be from any life event that throws you for an unexpected loop, leaving you feeling un-grounded or disconnected with yourself.

The messy middle is the space between the beginning and the ending of something, and it is that place where we do not feel like we have our bearings. On the one hand it is confusing, overwhelming, and can feel isolating. On the other, the messy middle is a place of transition and transformation (whether we like it or not). The messy middle is unsettling because we do not know what to expect, and it is a space of being in-between things. The messy middle can show up during things you have planned (home improvement projects) and in things you do not plan for yourself (pandemics, health issues, accidents, and the like). Brené Brown shares that , the messy middle is where "magic happens." And, even though the end point of what you are going through feels far away, and resolution is often much closer than think when we are in the mess of the middle.

How do we find joy in the messy middle?

In short, it is by being very present to your situation and your emotions and feelings about what is going on in your life. It takes staying on a path that is mindfully dedicated to joy. And it takes acknowledging your current circumstances.

While it sounds a bit woo-woo, I invite you to look at hardship and difficulty as an invitation to reconnect with joy and revisit the role it plays in our lives in a new way.

Joy is easy when times are good, and your life is going as you planned. Joy becomes a much more interesting proposal when you choose it when things are harder.

One of the key things about the messy middle is to notice that you are in it, and to *let it be messy*. Instead of jumping to judgement, or wishing that things would be different, look for to unpack whatever is going on for you. It takes time and action to work through the process and get through the middle of anything. The middle does not look "good" and it does not usually feel good, but you are also not at the end of things. Learning to sit with the discomfort of being in the middle, and to discovering ways to choose joy during that time is a part of the process.

I invite you to join me in being wholly present with your life right now. What does it look like, and what are you seeing in this messy middle time?

What feelings are you noticing? What is stressing you out? What do you know for sure?

The Messy Middle from a Spiritual Perspective

From a spiritual perspective, life's journey leads us straight into the messy middle many times. When you encounter personal hardships, or when you are working and sorting through trauma past or present, or when you find yourself in the ending phase of things, that is when the messy middle opens right up. And while the messy middle is the hardest place to find joy (sometimes) and it feels like the weirdest place to look for joy (every time), it is exactly the time when joy and reconnecting with your own wellbeing are the most important. Right there in the very inconvenient messy middle.

The messy middle is a time of transformation. You cannot have growth without growing, just as you cannot have a beginning or an ending without a middle. Each of us must go through something to get to the other side.

In one interview I had with Fred LeBlanc of the band Cowboy Mouth, he opened up about how he finds joy when he's feeling stuck. In the past he has faced a messy divorce, and financial hardships with his band. And he knows that playing the drums is a sure way to find his way back to what he loves. Drumming brings him joy. When he returns to the action of drumming, he is connected to joy, and it builds on itself.

Fred said that when he feels disconnected, or when he notices that he has let ego take over, he enjoys "the feeling of a drumstick in my hand," or feeling the power of hitting the drums. With small, mindfully chosen steps, he reconnects with his inner source and can move back into a place of joy and positivity. "I find ways of growing on joy, on the simple things."

Beware of the Spiritual Bypass and Toxic Positivity

Before we jump further into finding joy, I want to first address the messy middle we are currently living in. COVID-19 hit, and everything in our lives changed in 2020. Many of the activities that have brought us joy are no longer accessible to us. Many things that you and I felt were easy daily tasks are no longer easy or done daily.

As humans conditioned for "doing," it is easy to fall into one of two counter productive coping mechanisms as we sit with the discomfort of our current reality: looking for a silver lining in the midst of the messy middle (spiritual bypassing) or sharing memes that reflect a mindset of "good vibes only" (toxic positivity). This book does not embrace either of these mindsets, and actively encourages you dig deeper.

One the one hand: I am all for reflection and hopefulness. Escapism is great when done mindfully and intentionally. Hopefulness is important when times feel hard. And, remaining vigilant in one's pursuit of all things positive is important.

At the same time: jumping to the silver lining or focusing on what we all *might* learn from this situation in the future offers an easy side door to avoiding this place that is so uncomfortable. This is especially true when it is done in a casual way, or without any kind of self-reflection. Glossing over a situation, or not spending time with how it has impacted your life can be seen as spiritual bypassing, a term coined by John Welwood. He shares that this is the "tendency to use spiritual ideas and practices to sidestep or avoid facing unresolved emotional issues, psychological wounds, and unfinished developmental tasks."

The spiritual bypass is an important thing to be aware of because it is very easy to get caught up in it, and not even realize it. When you are in the midst of a hard thing, there's often the desire to get away from it. It is easy to share a sentimental meme on social media, which feels sweet for a moment.

Similarly, forcing a yourself into mindset of only allowing what is positive in your life is the mark of toxic positivity. It glosses over the truth of your situation, and pushes away the heart of what is going on in the messy middle. Feeling joy means that you also feel and encounter other emotions in your life. You can not have joy without also knowing sorrow. By only allowing good vibes, you are denying the fullness of the human experience. It denies part of your own existence, and more dangerously, leaves no room for the realness of depression or other mental health issues.

The heart of joy involves diving in, processing what is going on, and making a choice to reconnect with joy and embrace the truth of who you are. Shutting down difficult emotions does not honor all of the feelings you have based on the immensity of the situation. Let yourself feel what is going on. Find the support of a professional if you are feeling overwhelmed by the situation. While it feels scary, processing hard things opens up room for you to feel a deeper sense of well being and connection.

The Drummer, The Podcaster, and the Candlestick Maker

In addition to actively processing what is going on in hard times, it is also important to mindfully take action to reconnect with the things that you know bring you joy. Just like Fred LeBlanc, I am betting you can name several things that reconnect you to your own joy and deeper sense of self. Many of those things will be simple. Some take no more than a few moments to do. And all of them remain a practice, something you might drift away from time to time, but that you can return to when you feel messiness arise in your life.

Something I have learned from having a podcast all about joy since 2015 is that almost everyone can quickly reflect on several things that brought them joy as a child. And, nearly every one of them can find the ways that those things now play a role in their lives as adults. It is amazing to see the connections. The key is to recognize and name those times when you have felt inspired, and "in spirit," and to give yourself permission to reconnect with them. This creates a sacred through-line in your life, from your beginning to your current messy middle.

Someone who reflected on this through line in her life is Marsha Flowers. As a child, Marsha and her sister Lori used to play together using the nursery rhyme about the "butcher, the baker, and the candlestick maker" as inspiration. They would argue over who got to be the candlestick maker, and so it was no surprise to Marsha when she later discovered that it brought her great joy to create candles. As she observes, "It helps you to connect to that childlike wonder, to the joy of it. Right? I look back and go, 'Hey, I thought about doing this ....' even as a child I played with the idea. I can see those seeds way back. And I wonder how many people had those kinds of seeds planted early, and who aren't paying attention to what they're doing now, and how that tied in?" Today, Marsha is the owner of the delightful "Five Blessings Candles" that she started with her sister, where they create "Happiness in the Form of a Flicker."

The key for all three of us (the drummer, the podcaster, and the candlestick maker) is that we each got in touch with what inspired us, and we made the mindful intention to take real action towards bringing more of what we knew we loved into the world. Each of us followed our inspiration, and then made the mindful choice to take the actionable steps on that inspiration. We are connected to joy, and, connected to our own wholeness and purpose. We have found something that aligns with our spirit. This is the through line of what happens when we jump start joy.

When inner or outer chaos show up, you can take inspiration from these steps, too. The practice of staying close to joy is like a muscle; one you learn to flex it and get in touch with the joy that is at the center of who you are you will find that you can slow down, you can find joy more often, and you will feel more at ease in your life.

In good times, your joy can fuel and inspire others. In hard times, knowing what brings you joy and leaning into it can act as a driver to keep going, and provide you with a connection with something that is much bigger than yourself.

Finding Joy in the Messy Middle?

The first question I have asked every guest on my podcast since 2015 is: What brought you joy as a child? What were your earliest sparks of joy?

Where can you see the “seeds” of what was planted early in your life? Can you see the impact of that early joy on your life, now?

There are always clues for you to follow as to what helps connect you to your own sacred purpose and greater wellness. Joy is the mark of that sacred connection.

Using past joy as guidepost, what can you notice about what creates connection for you to your sacredness?

Taking inspiration from past joys, what action can you take to reconnect to that same joy in your life now?

If you're having trouble accessing those things for yourself, maybe you want to take inspiration from what I've seen as the top five answers from nearly 300 guests: nature, playing with animals, spending time with friends, creativity, and reading.

Honor that whatever you are facing right now is difficult. Often when we are faced with the discomfort of the messy middle, we find ourselves entering a lower stakes version of "fight, flight, or freeze." This is understandable. This can also cause us to numb out, or fight the reality of the situation, which can take a lot of mental and emotional energy. Acknowledge that this time is not easy, and it is taking energy for you to face it.

Fighting the reality of things often adds more pain to the truth of what is going on.
Instead of fighting or escaping, let yourself know that yes, you are in the middle of something messy, and yes, this too will pass.

Take inspiration from Pema Chodron's question: "What if instead of being disheartened by the ambiguity, the uncertainty of life, we accepted it, and relaxed into it?" Consider the things that may be out of your control but are creating stress for you. What can you let go of?

What might make it feel easier to accept the reality of what is happening?

CHAPTER THREE: Joy is a Choice

"Joy does not simply happen to us. We have to choose joy and keep choosing it every day."
- Henri Nouwen

In the midst of being caught up in "doing" (instead of "being"), many of us have lost our daily connection with joy and with our true selves. In the busy-ness of living, we often find ourselves pursuing "shoulds," or as Liz Gilbert describes it, "living someone else's dream." It is easy to forget that you are always in choice (which is another way of saying that you always have choices you can make: whether that be what to have for lunch, or which path to take on your next walk). Remembering that you have agency, and choices available to you in any moment are lifelines to joy and a feeling of freedom.

The issue is that we often forget that we have choices when inner or outer chaos hits. The fear that kicks up when we feel overwhelmed and ungrounded is one of the most overwhelming things about the messy middle. It is easy to abandon ourselves and our needs, because getting through hard times often means we tap into the "doing" side of our emergency management toolkit. Instead of taking the time to feel, we do. Instead of honoring our emotions, we hunker down and keep moving. This is noble, and honorable, and often what is realistically required in the moment.

At the same time, if we do not slow down, quiet the mind, and take the mindful action of choosing to listen to our own hearts, things start to feel even harder than they already are.

It is in these difficult situations, often when we feel the least connected, that I believe joy comes looking for us. Joy shows up, and reminds us of what we love, of what is important, and that we are always in choice. It floats us memories of our earliest sparks of connection, and it invites us to rediscover our own through lines. It whispers to us to return to ourselves. And it can be the most powerful thing we have ever witnessed.

In 2010, I experienced both the messiest of middles and I saw firsthand how joy can show up even when things are at their worst. After the birth of my son, I was diagnosed with Postpartum PTSD. And, with that came the very disorienting feeling that I could not connect with the joyful side of myself. At the heart of the situation, I wanted more than anything to be the hopeful, joyful, connected mother that I knew the tiny baby I had brought into the world deserved. I longed to be the person I had known for 38 years. But in truth, I was in a place where I did not recognize myself at all.

It was exhausting just making the phone calls to ask for help. It was hard telling strangers about what had happened and what I was feeling because it was still so new and raw and unprocessed. Finding the energy to keep asking for help when I felt completely lost was one of the hardest things I have ever had to do. Eventually I found my way to a therapist who was a great fit, and who told me that one day, I would need to share my story.

I now interpret that as a time when joy came looking for me. It reached out when I could not find my way, and it invited me into a dance. The tendrils of joy were there when I knew I was not myself and did not even know what that meant. Joy wanted me to remember who I was and re-embody that. Joy inspired me to work past and through the fear, and to work beyond my comfort zone. It led me to discover and listen to my own intuition, and to rediscover that I can trust myself.

The dance meant that I was part of the give and take. It was my intention to find help, it was ultimately my action that led me to find it. In addition to therapy, that dance of continuing to choose joy on a daily basis was part of what kept me going and to find a way to restore my sense of wellbeing and connection with the core of who I am. And I see that as the beginning of an amazing rebirth of my own spirit, and in the ways that I share and receive joy and love in my life.

I know that wherever you are on your own journey, choosing joy can make an impact on your path and your outcome. Choosing joy and looking for joy and following the inkling deep down that you need to do something just for yourself is one of the most powerful things you can do.

Choosing Joy is Revolutionary

It takes heart and courage to choose joy. It takes digging deep to acknowledge that you want to find your way back to being a joy filled person, because society will tell you that everything else is more important.

If in the midst of this moment and this current hardship, you find yourself thinking “this is situation is not acceptable,” or you know deep down that there’s something so much more than the day to day you're living, then joy is reaching out to you.

The great news is that joy is available to you at any time and any place. You can be in the midst of difficult situations or your life can be hard, and you can choose to see or find joy. And once you have really sat with the fear or the hardship or the heartache and noticed what is being awakened in you, you can move through those hard emotions and into something else.

When you choose joy after living in a hard place, you are waking up to the possibility of what can be. You are seeing that there is hardness, and you are choosing something else for your life. You are acknowledging that not everything is easy, that you can weather a storm, and that you are worthy and capable of joy.

Of course, this is not easy and as I shared about my own journey there is often a very real mental health aspect to reconnecting with oneself and one's joy. I am not suggesting that anyone can simply be happy if they set their mind to it. Returning to joy takes work. If you are inspired to mindfully take the steps to jump start your joy and your own wellness, your first action step may be to find support. I believe that you can have mental health challenges, and that part of following joy means that you become an advocate for yourself and active participant in finding your way back to wellness.

There is "coraggio" involved with choosing joy. My friend, Father Rusty likes to share that the Italian word for courage (coraggio) reflects that courage is a mix of both bravery, and heart. I know that choosing joy is takes embracing coraggio. You alone can choose to say that joy matters and your happiness matters, and that you matter. This takes courage and time. It takes remembering who you are, who you were, and reconnecting to that version of yourself. And it takes seeing new possibilities for your life, and the world.

What Henri Nouwen says about choosing joy is revolutionary: "Joy does not simply happen to us. We have to choose joy and keep choosing it every day." We have to choose it every day because the world and society has other ideas about who we are and what we should do. It is revolutionary to stand up and say that you are valuing your own joy and wellness.

The world around us will tell us that we are more valuable when we pursue profits and productivity. Many cultures have a stigma around what it means to encounter depression, PTSD, or other mental health challenges. And it is so extremely easy to listen to those outside voices, cultural norms, and stigmas. The problem is that we abandon our true selves when we don't listen to what our heart, and what joy, says we really need. This takes digging deep and choosing to go forth with coraggio: embracing the heart and courage of being joyful.

How to Jump Start Your Joy When You Feel Lost:

Snapshot moments. Think of a time when you had the sense that you were surrounded by joy. It might be a family gathering, a party, a vacation, or a time that you celebrated something you were proud of. It might also be a moment you noticed a flower, saw a hummingbird, or delighted in the large artichoke plant in your garden.

Think back to that snapshot and sink into that moment. What did you feel? What did you see, and smell? Who was there? What were you wearing? Allow yourself the gift of sitting in that for a few moments.

Think back to one of the times that you felt joy. Take 5 minutes to sit with that memory and relive it in detail if you can. Notice how you feel. Keep that as a place in your mind that you whenever you need to.

If you are feeling stuck, overwhelmed, or upset - what would inspire you to feel just a little bit better right now? What would move you one step closer to joy (even a tiny step), that you could take in this moment? What action can you take today or tomorrow to make that happen?

Listen, get quiet, and notice what little things the universe might be telling you and calling you towards. In my own journey back to joy, I found that there were little nudges and inspirations of the things to do to find my way back to well-being. From the unshakable inkling I needed to keep searching for the right kind of help, to seeing words and reminders pop up of the joy that I longed for, there were clues pointing me in the right direction.

If you are having a hard time, take the time to mindfully look and listen for the inspiration and universe's nudges of what is the next right step for you. Even if it feels scary or out of your comfort zone, make the step to the next easiest thing to do.

Bonus! What is your cornerstone quote or theme song? What quote helps remind you who you are, even in hard times? What song reminds you of your joyful and centered self? Think on both, and make a point to listen to your songs (or make a play list), and find a place to display your quote as a reminder of your connection to your own joy.

CHAPTER FOUR:
Planning for Joy

"In the planning stage of a book, don't plan the ending. It has to be earned by all that will go before it."
— Rose Tremain

In the time of COVID, we have everyone at home and our homes are working as the catch all location for our lives. It is easy to feel like time and space and even our own personal space has lost its form and its sacredness. With time feeling subjective, and there being less structure to our days, it is easy for everything to blend together or things to feel rushed or lost. Or both.

When I started out on life coach training, I found that it was easy to be overwhelmed with the number of things I was juggling. What I discovered was that if I wrote things down, on a single calendar (with my google calendar being the single catch all of work, class, podcasting, coaching, my son's commitments, my personal commitments, and anything my husband had that meant I needed to be on point for watching our son) then... I would get to it.

This led me to the observation that if something is not on my calendar, it is not going to happen.

And the same is true for joy. Too often, joy gets overlooked as a non-essential thing and one that we think just pops up from time to time.

We think of joy as something that happens at big events like birthdays and weddings, on trips, and on special days when you drop everything and go to the beach.

What do you notice about all those big, joyful things?

They are scheduled. You find a place on your calendar for them. You make room for them. And you look forward to them for days or weeks or a year as you get closer to them.

The same is true for smaller joys, and for everyday joys. You need to put time on the calendar to do something joyful, or light hearted, or restful, or it may not happen. And just like a big vacation that you can see on your calendar, it's a small joy to know that at 2pm on Thursday you're going to stop and do a puzzle with your kid, or take your dog to a new dog park, or treat yourself to a home manicure.

Planning for Joy

Yes, joy can unfold around us without any warning. Those are the moments of pure magic, when out of nowhere we see something that is so special and beautiful that we delight in being alive just to see it. Inspiration is much like joy, sometimes it "just hits" when you are working on a podcast episode, or a book, or any creative endeavor.

There is another way to access inspiration, and for joy. When I schedule time to sit down and brainstorm, write, and work on episodes for my podcast I have a much easier (and more joyful) time with the creative process than when I used to "wait for inspiration to hit" before starting to work. This means that I mindfully look for inspiration in the world around me, and set the intention to create a new episode, and then take the action of beginning work. With the inspiration, intention, action framework in place the ideas flow easier, books or quotes pop up around me in my life, and I can craft a show that feels like it came from a place of flow and ease.

There is something magical that happens when you say yes to something (either joy or a creative activity) and make room for it. That is when joy and creativity join you in your pursuit. They show up with you and engage in the dance of creation and happiness. Like any relationship, your relationship with joy needs time and space. Joy wants you to respect it and spend time with it.

And so, the way to make sure that you make room for joy and find it in your life regularly is to put it on your calendar.

Well Planned, Loosely Held

As you begin to mindfully align yourself with creating more joy in your world, it is important to consider the role that impermanence plays in our reality. I believe that how and when we allow ourselves to experience joy is tied to how we understand change in our lives.

As someone who has had experience in project management, and who dives into the spiritual and coaching side of things regularly, I see that there are two things that are constants in our lives, and that impact our expectations of how life should play out:

There are two truths about most people:
People love to plan and like to feel like they can control what is happening in their world.
People don't like the idea that things change, or that things might be out of their control.

There are two truths about how things unfold in life:
There's not much we can truly control. Control is an illusion.
Impermanence and change are two of the only things we can count on.

The disconnect between what most of us want (things to stay the same), and what actually happens (everything changes, even us!) is the source of a lot of heartache and pain because these two things do not co-exist together with ease. And it is when we fight to keep the illusion of our control alive that we end up with a lot of pain, and a lot of confusion, and it can pull us away from joy.

One way that I have found to balance these two desires is to move forward with a "Well Planned, Loosely Held" mindset. It means that you plan for what you want in your life and take actions on those plans. And it means that as things change, you evolve your plans. Instead of clinging tightly to how things were "supposed to be," it allows you the space to pivot, regroup, and re-envision your path. Evolution allows you to remain open to possibility and find the joy in your journey.

Finding Joy in The Now

Knowing that life is full of impermanence and learning to embrace change can shift your experience of the "messy middle." The way I see it is that life is a series of messy middles. And, life is also full of messiness, and full of seasons where we are in the middle of many things. Just as we have highs and lows at specific times and in certain seasons, I tend to feel like "the middle" is life, on the macro level. Life is always at least a little messy. It gets way messier sometimes than others. Sometimes we can see when we are really having a difficult time and need help to find our way out of the mess.

Part of being able to jump start and maintain joy means being able to look at both "messy" and "middle" in new ways. In the midst of hardship, it's not uncommon to say (or hear other people say) things like, "Everything will be better when..." or "I'll be happy when..."

This kind of thinking means that you are pushing joy aside, to an undetermined date in the future. It might mean that you are also denying yourself a connection with your own deeper truths and putting the pressures of the world ahead of what you need for yourself. That is not to say that logistically, some of these statements are true: in the case of the pandemic, it's true that there are things we will be able to DO again when restrictions are lifted. It is also true that most of us need to work, clean the house, and fill our gas tanks.

The problem with linear thinking is that they keep you trapped from experiencing joy, and from experiencing a deeper connection to your inner source in the moment. It denies your connection to yourself, your self expression, and your own truths. These thoughts stop you from allowing yourself to feel good when things are hard.

The shift here is more about looking at how you want to BE, and how you want to feel, in the midst of other difficult things and situations. This may mean that you need to give yourself the permission to feel joy regardless of what else is going on. You deserve to feel joy, and your joy is not dependent on the perfect set of circumstances to arise for joy to be an "appropriate" feeling.

Instead of thinking of things in a linear way (that things are either/or), consider looking for the "and." Things can feel bad now, and you can also choose joy. You can feel messy, and your mess can be joyful. You can be in shelter in place and find ways to connect.

We all encounter highs and lows as we go through life, with some of them being much more stressful and overwhelming than others. Once you have learned to jump start your joy, you will find that joy and a connection to yourself becomes accessible to you, no matter the situation. Whether you are having a good day, or a bad day, you will be able to access joy.

Maintaining joy in your life is an active practice. Choosing joy means it is a daily event, and it takes maintenance throughout your life. And I love that the word maintenance has the same root as the French word "maintenant" which means "now." We can start to think of the maintenance of choosing joy as something we do now. Not when things are "better," not when things change, but now.

Some Steps to Take When Scheduling Time for Joy

Take inspiration from the idea of "Maintenant," or "now." Do you have self-imposed boundaries or limitations as to when it is "appropriate" to feel or experience joy in your life? Do you find yourself saying things like, "I'll be happy when..."? Is this true? Are there ways that you could be happy now?

Allow yourself to want something more than what is real for you in this moment. If you are feeling pain or grief, give yourself permission to also feel joy or happiness about something else in your life. As humans we are often under the impression that if we are mourning, we cannot also have joy. This is not true. Each of us is very capable of holding two emotions at once. Give yourself permission to feel joy. Acknowledge that you desire to feel joy, and that it is important to you now.

Are there times where joy is allowed, and other times when you feel like it is not allowed, or you need to keep joy bottled up?

Block off time on your master calendar, a couple of hours a week, for something fun or joyful. As you block off the time, think of something that would feel joyful for you for the amount of time you have.

Try out a joyful "Ten in Three" exercise if you are having a hard time figuring out new things that you can do and that may feel great right now. To do this, set a timer for 10 minutes and on a piece of paper, write out all the things that bring you joy. Write as fast as you can and get as many as you can on to the page. Next, choose ten of these things that you can do over the next three months. Choose things that work within the reality of what you know the next three months will bring (take into consideration weather, health, other things that you have planned). Make a point to plan these joyful activities or events in. Hold on to your list so you can refer to it in the future.

CHAPTER FIVE: Joy Does Not Just Happen To You

Joy is an inside job. On we start to attune to it, joy flows forth more easily and more freely. And not only do we see more of it, but we give more of it.

I remember being in high school and having a very pivotal conversation with my mom around the time I was applying to college. I was having a hard time acknowledging my role in my accomplishments. It may have been that I was resistant to owning my role in the things I'd done, or, it could be that I had so thoroughly enjoyed doing some of the things (drama and softball come to mind) that I didn't see them as work.

Either way I had a really hard time listing them out, and remember vividly blurting out, "I didn't DO any of that, those things just happened to me." And my mom said, "No, you made all of those things happen. You brought them to life."

Joy is a lot like this. You may not see that you have an active role in bringing joy into your life, because those things feel authentically connected to who you are. It is possible that you feel like you can remember joyful times, but do not feel like you have a role in them or brought them about.

I've come to understand that there are two different kinds of joy: the kind we create from an organic perspective in our lives (which may feel easy to us), and the kind that I call "Bed in a Bag" versions of joy (which are created for us to enjoy).

These kinds of joy have a lot in common: they are joy filled, they can be immersive, and you can schedule time for them in your lives. The collective net gain from both is joy.

I want to be careful and say this about both types of joy: I am not labeling either type of joy "good" or "bad." I am not saying one is better than the other. I am inviting you to take a look at these two kinds of joy so that you can dive deeper into your experience of joy in your life. If something brings you joy, I want you to embrace that thing and fully allow yourself to experience the joy that it brings you. I have enjoyed many "Bed in a Bag" versions of joy, and I can see the impact they have on my lives and the lives of others.

Break Beyond of the Bed in a Bag Version of Joy

Bed in a Bag versions of joy are the easy, done for you, pre-packaged joy-filled events and situations that require virtually no planning and are socially accepted as places or times for joy. We go to these places to escape, enjoy, and soak in good times. Some examples of a "Bed in a Bag" version of joy are theme parks, cruises, movies, bouncy house places, pop up events made for Instagram-able photos, done for you birthday parties, subscription boxes. Generally, you pay, and you receive a thing or an event that is carefully curated to bring you joy.

With these events and situations, all we do is show up, or pay, and we've got a "Bed in a Bag" approach to happiness (just as you'd go to purchase the sheets, comfortable, pillows, shams and bed skirt that all match and provide an easy update to your bedroom).

These are great, and I also want to call them what they are: a prepackaged, consumable approach to joy that's appealing because it takes the legwork and planning out of the equation and drops you straight in the middle of the fun. And while it's great for some situations, and there's a time and a place for them (I'm a big fan of cruises and theme parks), it's easy for them to become our go-to for happiness. Many of them take place in ways that are total escapism, without any sort of integration with our day to day lives. So instead of finding and creating joy in our lives in the here and now, we have become used to leaving our normal lives to go somewhere else for immersive fun, instead of weaving fun into our daily existence.

Here is an example from my own life: In the first Season of my podcast I interviewed Danny Wood of New Kids on the Block. That conversation shifted many things in my life. It reminded me of my love of 80s music, and it offered a connection point with my sister that re-energized our relationship.

Since then, my sister and I have gone on two New Kids on the Block cruises. Were these "Bed in a Bag" versions of joy? Yes. That said, by saying yes to those trips, I tapped into things I did not realize were missing in my life.

I feel that we need to bust through the walls of "Bed in a Bag" versions of joy for a couple of reasons. First, these kinds of pre-packaged versions of joy may not be accessible to you when you are in the messy middle. Some of this is logistics: during a pandemic many things shut down, or if you are in emergency mode because of a non-pandemic messy middle you are likely to become focused on what is necessary in the moment. In those situations, you are not in a place where you can make time to visit a theme park or go to the movies. The other reason is that you need reclaim and learn to use your own joy-making muscles so that you are able to access joy wherever you go, and no matter what you encounter.

What is Missing?

In looking back at my own experience on the cruise, I noticed that there were things missing from my daily life that had once been a very real part of who I am. I delighted in a renewed connection with my dear sister, in the unbridled exuberance of 2500 people dancing on a Lido deck with a boy band, in the community of fans, and in the creativity of planning for theme parties.

I would never have guessed that a cruise with a boy band would have ever been a pivotal or transformational experience for me. And yet, there it was. Saying yes to doing something for joy's sake allowed me to participate in, and name, qualities of joy and connection that I wanted more of in my life.

This is one of the links in the chain of joy: You must take the first step towards whatever will light you up, and let joy take you on the journey. You have to tap into "coraggio" and play into "well planned, loosely held," and see what unfolds for you. I could have judged what going on the cruise meant, or judged my own taste of music. That would have stopped me from going. I think many of us do this every day: we stop ourselves from enjoying something because of some reason that resides outside of ourselves. We let judgements limit our experience.

This judgement is not limited to boy band cruises; we do this on all sorts of things. This could be going to a retreat, to spending a day on a beach, to taking a nap, to getting a pet dog, or painting a wall in your home. We stop ourselves from doing or having what seems joyful to us with excuses that keep us reigned in and stop us from expressing what we really want to do.

When we say yes to what the universe sends our way, and embrace whatever it has to teach us, we grow. We learn about what reconnects us with joy. And we learn what was missing before when we reconnect with what is true for each of us. There are places in each of our lives where we have lost touch with what brings us joy and been focused on being reactive to the world around us. "Bed in a Bag" versions of joy offer an amazing opportunity to look at what lights us up, and notice where there have been gaps in our everyday life.

The messy middle also offers an interesting time to notice what you want more of in your life, because you are thrown into a time that feels especially hard. In the last year, you may have noticed that you want more connection, more freedom, more space... the list will be different for each person.

With most of these things not available to us during a pandemic, it offers the opportunity to look for good old-fashioned versions of joy.

In reflecting on a past experience, noticing what is missing, and noticing what you wish could be offer two profound ways to acknowledge ways that joy can play a bigger role in your life.

Re-Entry and Integration

For many years, I led retreats at San Damiano Retreat in Danville, California. At the end of each retreat, we talked about "re-entry," or what happens when people return to their everyday life.

When you go on a retreat, you are mindfully separating yourself from the rest of life and given a beautiful container with which to explore your own deeper truths. You meet people who doing something similar. Re--entry can be rough.

The key to navigating re-entry is through integrating what you've learned, and finding a way to keep in touch with them on a daily basis. For retreatants, that might be developing a meditation practice or remembering that you felt especially connected while journaling.

Integration is a key part of joy, as well. After going on a cruise or experiencing an amazingly joyful time at a "Bed in a Bag" version of joy, it is important to notice what lit you up. Ask yourself why that brought you such joy. And then, instead of letting that event take place outside of your day to day life, find a way to integrate it.

Integration is a powerful way of choosing joy. It says to yourself and to the universe, and to others that these kinds of "fun" and joyful things matter to you. It means you are connecting with joy and exuberance daily or weekly.

It is far too easy to experience joy and let it stay "over there" and outside your daily routine. It is exactly what we have been taught: to compartmentalize every part of our life, and we often think that joy and our enjoyment of life is bound by a similar kind of thinking.

Joy can be the thing that is interwoven in your life, nearly everywhere. You can choose to have joy at work, at play, on your walk, and in your commute. You can infuse joy everywhere, in everything, and with nearly everyone you meet. Joy is not a singular, personal thing, but rather a collective experience. Your joys grow on each other, and feed other people. Choosing joy and aligning with the wellness that joy brings is a practice that involves embracing abundance and leaning into trust. When you integrate the things that light you up into your life, it allows you to experience your own wholeness, and the wholeness of the planet in a new way.

Here is how to approach this:

When have you felt most centered, connected, and loved in your life? What kinds of things have you done that let you slip into "the zone," where time and space slow down and you feel energized? (Drama and softball were two for me, that were obviously hard work but only felt like play). Did you, or do you, recognize those as a connection with joy? Why or why not?
In looking at past or present "Bed in a Bag" events: What about them felt joyful? What did they connect you to, in a deeper way?

When you are in the messy middle, you might notice the void of those things before you can name exactly what is missing from your life. If you like theme parks, or concerts, what are they connecting you to in a universal way? There is something sacred to notice about what they connect you with: hospitality, love, community, creativity, and more than likely: love and joy.

In considering both your "organic" joys, and your "Bed in a Bag" versions of joy, what lies in the crossroads of both? For me, there's community, creativity, and connection involved in both.

If you are feeling stuck, how can you work more of the key values you've identified into your life?

CHAPTER SIX:
The Joy of 'Playing Small'

"The place to start is, why do you want to do this? Why do you want to bother about this? Why do you want to put the time and energy and learning into it? Start there." – Jennifer Louden

Joy comes in many shapes and sizes. As people living in today's world, it's easy to think of joy as things that come with big, celebrated events. And it is easy to have set ideas about what joy looks like, what it sounds like, or when joy should take place.

I invite you take a new look at this and try on the lens of what it means to "play small." I am not suggesting that you shrink yourself, or shirk responsibilities, or hide out. Playing small is not the opposite of "Playing Big." It means focusing on the small things that bring us the most joy, along with allowing ourselves to take joy in the small things.

I remember feeling very conflicted by my traditional career path after my son was born. On the one hand I felt there were expectations that I "should" want to continue to climb the corporate ladder and keep working on bigger and bigger advertising clients at bigger and bigger advertising agencies. The pressure was on to learn more, do more, work harder, work longer, and I often felt that I needed to sideline my family and the joy I felt with them in order to prioritize work.

It didn't feel like there was a lot of room or acceptance from society around slowing down and wanting to be a mom for a while, let alone an understanding of what it meant to have a small child at home. There were plenty of subtle and (not so subtle) messages and attitudes in corporate settings that made it clear some people believed that working from home meant I was probably slacking off, that leaving to pick up a child from day care was a conflict of interest, or that taking a full week off was allowed by policy but in reality, it was frowned upon. I found that I did not like it one bit, and I found that I felt really conflicted about not liking it.

It took me a long time to accept that wanting to spend time with my son and start a business that allowed me to spend more time at home (instead of in an office) and cuddle my dog was OK. It took some time to embrace that wanting to leave room and space in my life for the people that mattered was a noble thing. And, eventually I came to see that choosing these things was more than OK: it is honorable and beautiful, joyful, important, and sacred.

I have come to call honoring your decisions and doing what matters most to you "Playing Small." It stems from a place of embracing the small things that matter a lot. Playing small means that you value the little things, and the tiny moments, and the beauty that sits in them. These moments hold tiny glimpses into what is sacred for you, what connects you to others, and what connects you with the universe on a larger level.

Playing Small means choosing the unconventional things that matter to you, even when they do not matter to others. It means you get to embrace what feels right to you, right now, and you can change your mind about it all later, too. Playing small means finding what fits into your life, at this stage and optimizing your life around your choices. Playing small means that you decide what is important, you decide how much time you will spend on it, and it means trusting yourself.

The first step is admitting to yourself that you want the thing that seems "unconventional." It means you admit that you woke up and said, "you know, I've worked hard at my career and now I want something else. That is scary and weird, and not what I expected, but I can't change what my heart wants, and I'm going to follow it."

Once I had taken the steps to following my heart and intuition, everything shifted into a far more joyful place. I stopped fighting the reality of what was hard (I couldn't stand being in a corporate setting, which was likely fueled by me wishing I was doing something else), and started saying yes to the things that felt right to me. It no longer mattered if it was right to society. But when I stepped into that space, things fell into place.

Playing small lets us move out from under the things you are hiding from, and step into the full light of what you want, what brings you joy, and what lights you up. It means you get to embrace your heart and your desires.

How to Play Small

My friend Father Rusty tells a story of when he was discerning his path. His mentor asked him to tell him the deepest yearning of his soul. Father Rusty would come back week after week with a new answer, each of which the mentor would nod and say, "That's not it! Go deeper!!"

Finally, Rusty came back with this answer, “To dance and to share in the dance with others.” And that was it. That is his purpose and his joy.

Try peeling back the layers of what is your heart's deepest yearning. What are you here to do? Keep going until you have got something that feels right, on a soul level. Be your own mentor and encourage yourself to keep digging deeper.

Love or fear? When I was learning to trust my own intuition and re-calibrate getting to know what brought me joy, I had a question I’d ask myself before every decision: Am I doing this thing from a place of love, or fear? If I could whole heartedly answer “love,” than it was a go.

If I answered fear, or fear of something (being judged, FOMO, looking dumb), then I had to rethink the answer. Give it a go and see what happens.

What are you afraid to admit to yourself, about what you know you want? What could be possible if you said yes to that thing?

CHAPTER SEVEN: Joy for Joy's Sake

The 'gap moment' is that tiny moment in time in between when something happens, and when you react. In the gap moment, you are always in choice.

Even when things feel really hard, and you are knee deep in the messy middle, you still have choices. And those choices revolve around the steps of inspiration, intention, and action mindset that started early in this book.

You can choose to look for inspiration from other people who have been through something similar, either now or in the past.

You can choose to be mindful in how you interact in any situation and how you talk to yourself about it. Instead of being angry or judgmental, you can choose to be curious or remain open to hearing or learning more.

You can mindfully choose to wait to be emotionally involved in a situation until you have more answers.

You can choose to surrender to what is happening instead of placing yourself in fight mode if the situation doesn't involve immediate danger.

You can choose to take steps to make your situation just a little bit better, or to make it better for other people.

You can use the "I am I doing this from a place of love or fear" question to determine what is informing your decision to react in any given way.

The hard thing is that when you are in the messy middle, fear wants you to believe that you are stuck. And that is fear talking. Fear wants you to feel stuck, and not make choices. It tells you that you are safer here, in the known situation than you are "over there" where there are unknowns. Knowing that, and acknowledging that, can help you realize that you do have other options.

Perspective and Horizons

One of the truths about the messy middle is that the horizon feels very close. It feels like you cannot see your options and that you are stuck.

A while back I was on vacation with my family at a home we rented near the ocean. I watched and delighted in the fog, as it came in and changed the view from our windows. When it was sunny out, we could see all the way to the ocean. But when the fog came in, we could only see to the hedgerow of trees near the house.

It struck me that the fog and the weather is like the change that we encounter in life. It comes in and changes the view. The horizon feels close when the fog comes in, just like our world feels close and too constricting when we are in the messy middle.

The thing is, just like the weather, you get to decide how you interpret any given situation. This is not looking for a silver lining. This is deciding how you want to approach it and choosing perspective over fear. If it has become difficult to see your way through the fog or the messy middle, these are the times to look for inspiration to act as a light to lead you through the fog.

And I liken that light filled inspiration to joy acting as a wayfinding emotion.

Joy is a Wayfinding Emotion

Joy is one of the highest vibrational emotions. It is transitory and sometimes fleeting, and it is hard to stay IN joy for long. That said, I often say that if you aim for joy and keep your sites on it, you will land in the realm of happiness, contentment, and peace even if you don't hit joy. And, when you focus on joy, you also begin to align yourself with your inner source, your purpose, and your own wholeness as a human being.

How can you use joy as a wayfinding emotion?

Make it a focal point in your thoughts. When you can, make it a point to look for the joy that is happening all around you. Notice the moments that are joyful.

Be mindful of things in your frame of reference, even if they are a "normal" part of your existence. Notice when the sky is blue, when you hear a bird singing, or notice the amazing intricacies of a flower.

When you feel a deep sense of contentment, whether that be in a conversation with another person, or in spending time with others, or in a moment in a movie, or in how the light hits the water, allow yourself to feel that feeling of peace and joy. Set the intention to notice and take a mental note for yourself in the moments that you see those things.

Make the effort to do things that are joyful, peaceful, and affirming. If you have a habit of say, playing video games, but you don't necessarily like how it makes you feel, find something to replace that habit or find a way to pivot it so that it feels good to you.

Let go of things that are not allowing you to feel good, or that you do out of a feeling of obligation.

Take a look at your work and your dreams. Do they align? While it might not be easy to make a change right this moment, what else can you do to bring joy into your life? Can you take a class, or start a side business or a creative endeavor that would allow you to spend more time doing something you love?

Find people who make you feel alive and energized and spend more time with them.

Joy for Joy's Sake

As we close out this tiny book, I invite you to take the things you have learned and dive into them in new ways. If you have found new inspiration in the reading or writing you have done, set the intention to continue the work of bringing joy into your life in an actionable way. Look at the places you have felt joy may be missing and create a plan to integrate those joys into your life.

It is my wish that you find small and meaningful joy filled moments in your everyday life. I also hope that you have rediscovered and reconnected with the things that brought you joy as a child, and that you find time to bring those into your life, now. Your joy is a connection to what is sacred and true for you like nothing else is.

I hope that you will set aside time to honor what joy is calling you to do. This may mean you set aside time just for yourself, to read, to watch a movie you love, or cuddle your dog, or to play a game with your family. It may mean you decide to start a podcast or write a book for no other reason than you have always wanted to start a podcast or write a book. Or it might look like saying yes to the possibly unconventional things that you know bring you joy, and that you value deeply.

In the beginning, following the nudges of inspiration you feel into action may feel frivolous, and without a direct purpose. You might not like the idea of doing something that does not feed a specific goal (and that might feel weird or foreign to you). You might feel uncomfortable with the idea of playing for the sake of playing, or that playful action is only "supposed" to happen on vacations, at theme parks, or at parties - in other words, that joy is reserved for special occasions and designated times.

Joy may also be nudging you to look at hard things in a new way, and that might feel uncomfortable. You may have realized that your next steps will led you into new territory for your life. Set judgement aside as you mindfully build the actionable steps for whatever is next for you. We have all been socialized to believe that valuable action is the kind that leads to an output or monetary gain, and that happy people look, act, and behave certain ways. It started early .. with those same old men at your dad's company picnic telling you that "happy" was not the right answer to their question about what you wanted to BE when you grew up. (and if you did not run into those guys you likely ran in to others). In your journey to mindfully reconnect with joy, the whole point is to BE, and reconnect with the childlike wonder of the world around you.

What I have found is that when you say yes to joy and start to take the steps to bring more of it into your life, it grows. Joy begets more joy. Curiosity and wonder create more joy. When you jump start your own joy, it jump starts the joy of those around you. Being in connection with your true nature, and in connection with spirit is important. Being connected with joy means that you are also connected with your true self, and that you are able to inspire and uplift others. And that is truly the greatest gift you can give them, and yourself, and the world.

Set up Your Beacons for Joy:

List out five things you can see as joyful in this moment. They can be small, or big things you are grateful for.

Practice using joy as your destination. At some point today, or this week, when you notice that you are feeling annoyed, upset, or overwhelmed, make a point to change what you are doing. Mindfully notice the emotion that comes up, whether it be anger, annoyance, irritation, etc. Allow yourself to see that you have been triggered in some way. Then, change whatever you are doing. Step outside for a walk if you are working at your desk. Pause a conversation if you are speaking with someone, and it is getting tense. Put down your phone if you have read something that is not aligned with what you feel passionately about, or that has upset you. And then, make the choice to do something that points to creating more joy in the world. That might be that you simply do not hit send on an email or that you do not add a comment to a conversation on Facebook.

Try a centering prayer meditation. This is different than sitting quietly, in silence. It is more of a mental exercise, acknowledging that thoughts arise and we each have a choice to acknowledge them and let them go. You can find my example of how to do this meditation here: https://bit.ly/centeringjoy

Revisit your Ten in Three, and your list of things that brought you joy as a child. Work one of those things into your day. Return to the things that are unique to you, and bring you joy. Let yourself appreciate and be renewed by them.

Choose Joy
By Paula Jenkins

I don't think our generosity or goodness
Our badness or stinginess
Causes time to pass quicker or slower
Time will come whether we choose joy or anger
Bitterness or hope

During sleep or waking
Time marches on, no matter

But for the human
What we choose for our time matters
Choosing joy every day
Makes hard times happier
Time is packed with more meaning
And our hearts remember our most important connections

Acknowledgements

This book has been a labor of love, and its pages have been impacted by many people in my life. Thank you to:

My mother Sally: for instilling in me a love of language and a curiosity about my world. And for being my editor.
My father Jim: for teaching me about philosophy, instilling in me a love of the audio arts, and believing that I could do anything I set my mind to.
My sister Sara: for being an inspiring source of joy in my life.
My son Zachary: for being my greatest teacher, and for carrying on the tradition of joy in our family.
My husband Sean: You are my rock and I love our family and our life together. Kay + Dapp 4ever.
Tammy, Stephanie, and Cris: Go Gauchos! Thank you for the humor and the love, and the years of companionship.
Kath: for YDS, sharing about the joy you have found in the chaos, and being my #1 podcast guest.
Michelle W: Thank you for pointing me always in the right direction and kicking my butt.
Julie, Liz, Kate, Valerie, Lara and TeamCLCC: for your profound impact in my life and holding space for me to BE.
Aimee and Christy, and all my podcasting clients: for believing in me and trusting me with your voice and message. I adore you.
Fred LeBlanc and Marsha Flowers, thank you for saying yes and for being on the show.
San Damiano Retreat, Father Rusty, and Sister Michelle.
Alexandra Franzen and Lindsey Smith: for the Tiny Book Class.
Mentors I have not met: Liz Gilbert, Brené Brown, Boy George, Pema Chodron and two that I have: Wayne Dwyer and Ram Dass.

The many podcast guests: You have changed my heart and taught me so many things about joy and your wisdom is woven in the words of this book.
The listeners and community around Jump Start Your Joy: I would not have a podcast without you, and I cherish each of you who tunes in and listens and shares your life and days with me.

If you have felt inspired by this book and want to find more ways to jump start joy in your life, in the world, and in other people's lives, I invite you to subscribe to my podcast:
Jump Start Your Joy.

You can also find out more at:
Website: Jumpstartyourjoy.com
Instagram: jumpstartyourjoy
Facebook: jumpstartyourjoy
Pinterest: jumpstartjoy
Twitter: jumpstartjoy

www.ingramcontent.com/pod-product-compliance
Lightning Source LLC
Chambersburg PA
CBHW030106070426
42448CB00037B/1210